Gallery Books
Editor Peter Fallon
DEVOTION

Mícheál McCann
DEVOTION

Gallery Books

Devotion
is first published
simultaneously in paperback
and in a clothbound edition
on 17 May 2024.

The Gallery Press
Loughcrew
Oldcastle
County Meath
Ireland

www.gallerypress.com

*All rights reserved. For permission
to reprint or broadcast these poems,
write to The Gallery Press:*
books@gallerypress.com

© Mícheál McCann 2024

The right of Mícheál McCann to be identified as Author of this Work has been asserted in accordance with Section 77 of the Copyright, Designs and Patents Act 1988.

ISBN 978 1 91133 870 3 *paperback*
       978 1 91133 871 0 *clothbound*

A CIP catalogue record for this book
is available from the British Library.

Devotion receives financial assistance
from the Arts Council of Ireland.

Contents

Song page 11

John 20:15 13
Adoration (Rhesus Disease) 14
Poet and Cat 15
Líadan Attests Her Love 17
At the Rondanini Pietà I Consider My Mother's Mother 19
Personal Poem (Pietà) 21
Darren Bradshaw's Last Drink 22
Haircut with Beard Trimmer 23
Auden's You 24
Elegy 25
Keeper 27
Encounter 28

Keen for A— 30

Sheep Chorus, Lisheegan 65
Swimming Off Snave Pier 66
Offshore Wind Farm 67
In a Lover's Family's Company 69
Late Blight 70
Devotion
    1 ROMANCE OPTION 71
    2 WHY THE CAT MEANS WHAT IT DOES 72
    3 ENVOI 74
    4 IMPROMPTU EVENING 75
    5 LOVE POEM 76
20s 77
How We Got Here, Where We're Going 78
Being Naked with Strangers 80
Travelling Poem 81
To an Imagined Child 82
Walking Through Empty Houses 83
Unaccompanied Walk 87

Acknowledgements and Notes 89

*for those who could
not name their love*

It seemed to me that what perished need not also be lost.
— Marilynne Robinson, *Housekeeping*

Song

*The quiet roll of the drum
of the washing machine,
some residual heat giving
from the long radiator
against my backside.
How a rose opens more
and more as it dies, wanting
to share one more thing.
To think I once volunteered
to eschew all this music.
The washing machine roars
through the thick walls
as the first day of winter
catches light like a dusty photograph
you blow on. The motes lift off,
smile-inducing. I persist
regardless, against all advice.*

John 20:15

Had I personally returned from death
corporeal, raging, I would have run
to find my shivering wispish lover,
not even dressing my naked form first
in limp rags or bevelled palm fronds.

Yet he stayed by the yawning mouth
of his tomb (so the story goes) pruning
fuchsia or cotton thistles. Why else
would he be mistaken for a gardener?
Here the dead tend their graves for visitors . . .

Were it that we inhabited our bodies newly
each morning and then could recognize
our last day simply: soil clumps falling
from our fingers as we turn to face
the woman calling and calling our name.

Adoration (Rhesus Disease)

Stubborn to a fault, sowing seeds of trouble
prior to life even starting, and situated belligerently
(if you'd believe) the wrong way in the womb,
it was my blood that did the trick, incompatible.

If only I had got the memo then, saved myself
the cut knees, the crescent scars on my hands.
My mother asks why I don't write about her —
she gave me her eyes, fingers for music —

and I hear the earnest note behind the poke.
I write the things I am trying to forgive, I say,
and consider my original sin: joining hands
with my mother across the canal of our knowing.

Grasping for a hand, to agglutinate. If only
I had waited, perhaps never emerged at all.
This weighted blood, thrumming as I write,
protests that notion in refusing to stay still.

Oh mother and brother of the flaming hair,
forgive me; I repent to the clock of the egg-timer
and the black cat demanding his meaty slop.
I only wanted a companion to share words with.

The prayer through the night of my blood —
that she gave, that he survived —
aches against the limits of my tired skin
as though to return to that beginning place

where love is close by, and any pain kissable.

Poet and Cat

for Leontia Flynn

Me and Pangur Bán work away
absorbed completely in our tasks.
His whole being leans to play
while I peel apart fusty words.

Oh, respite from ass kissers,
my lamplit evenings, not talking.
This noir cat has his own matters
to attend to (mainly mousing).

It's quite quiet, this small flat
with us in it, awfully monkish
and having a solid go at
this or that, always fishing.

Often mice hang between his paws;
less often I seize
on the exact word or phrase
for our unruly ways.

He directs his copper eyes
to the yellow walls. Meanwhile,
reluctant, I fix mine
on the still blank page. Sigh.

He bravely displays medals
(rodents) in toothy rapture;
if a stanza stops rebelling
I grin at its capture.

This is the story of days:
our easy agreement, two crafters

joined in some verbal play.
Our work is never finished.

Prayerful practice
made this feline a virtuoso.
My thoughts sharp as his scratch.
Together we peer from the window.

from the 9th-century Irish

Líadan Attests Her Love

Her love continued on with his life, settling elsewhere. She sought him out in an unfamiliar townland of beautiful flowers, and said to whoever listened:

Awful is the thing
that I have done:
to wound the one I love.

Were it not for glares regarding my conduct
I could never have resisted
what Cuirithir wanted of me.

His desire was understandable,
to reach a heavenly place together
and forget any sort of pain.

It was over a foolish matter that I hurt him.
My hands grow gentle and tender
as they near his face.

I am Líadan.
I loved and love him.
This is the truest thing I can say.

We were companions over a time
that seemed to pass quickly.
We were close.

On one side of our walks were the sounds
of the great forest (curlews remind me of him),
on the other, the lulling sea.

Were it that no aspect of me
could hurt this fortress of a man,
gone elsewhere now.

Write it! — He was my heart, a soft wind
through the hedge outside, even though
I should commit my love to all rather than just one.

A chill has taken up in me . . .
and without his company
I cannot love.

from the 9th-century Irish

At the Rondanini Pietà I Consider My Mother's Mother

1

The art guide becomes Shakespearean, orating that the Virgin
is reunited with the Divine; how Cicero was inspired by this.

A vaulted room is painted ochre yellow in Italian sunshine.
Snatches of *Art History 101* reach me at the group's rear end.

The personification of Divine Providence . . . serene expressions
indicate *pietà* despite *humanitas* . . . A sense of surrender

and blessèdness overtakes the scene. Crossing the threshold
to the gallery proper a hush falls over the tour group.

2

An unfinished quality to them, as though Michelangelo fled
outside to buy chilled milk. Had he plans to return?

Mary holds her nude child upright with considerable effort.
The twist in her mouth, the downturned calm of his face.

Such agony scored into beautiful stone is not so alien
a prospect these days. A sliver of sun highlights his side.

3

What I see is a mother holding the lifeless body of her child,
keeping him vertical as though to puppet him back to life.

What I hear is a woman with a Northern accent and a boy
who didn't know his life had started. Agony in the garden.

In this version I see the mother pound the soggy earth
as she hears soldiers pass, raiding another house,

killing another woman's son. Her arms refuse to tire
stuffing pages of torn novenas into bottles of sloshing whiskey.

It is said that the love of a child can explain much.
It is said that she watched the fire for a very long time.

Personal Poem (Pietà)

My hometown boasts no shortage of them —
the broad vowels of a mother's voice break
over the athletic but emaciated body of a son.
To think I nearly inflicted this on her.

Darren Bradshaw's Last Drink

There are three religions in Northern Ireland — Catholic, Protestant, and gay.

The smell of poppers is almost atmospheric,
some say. It's the freest place in Belfast,
say others. The Parliament's exterior generic
enough — olive bricks, black-grill bars

on the windows belie the lights, the lights
that ricochet off people with no concerns
for the evening. Lisburn lesbians
rubbing shoulder pads with Shankill lesbians,

and one bar-stool drinker, a little apart
from the others. Dance music was bleeding
into the awful Friday night air outside.
No one knows if it was lager or a G&T,

if any of the bullets hit his glass too, if
'It's Alright' was playing as the aux was pulled.

Haircut with Beard Trimmer

By halves I do not do things,
so this windowless bathroom becomes
a musky masculine-smelling salon:
towels rolled, toilet rolls stowed,
a starling-blue facecloth draped over
the thin radiator, warmly, to sculpt
around your neck. You reverse cowboy

the toilet seat and I set to work.
An untrained Brutalist, gently hacking
unsubtle gaps in a burgeoning scalp
where blue veins, like curious dolphins,
threaten to approach the surface.
I am the assistant playing games

as the tired master eats some lunch.
And yet to hold a head heavy with duty
whose curls tighten with weariness . . .
The fuzzy loops of you fall to the tiles
like duck tears, or rain against a window,
muted, as all things are, in those
first few bright moments of wakening.

Auden's You

Stranger, though the night is gone,
I still recall the stain of it,
awake as we were throughout.
The dark comfort of the a.m.
which softened to a dull grey,
the Dublin mountains
were snow-tipped.
Us pretzel-like.

A bare room for the night
and I made you glad,
you me glad.
The clock stopped going
as the morning approached.
Time dammed its water flow.
I lost myself, forgot perils,
and for that I am grateful.

That this happened so long ago
the nuance of your humour
is long gone.
And yet this memory.
The one jigsaw piece
I cannot throw away.
A glorious portent
of ongoing, of being glad.

Elegy

Saint Buadan's Boat — emerald today
with seaweed — has as little luck
as this gelatin flotilla marooned
along the length of the strand.

Waterbirds and pine martens
observe from the grey sky
and lonely dunes respectively.
Do they wonder as I do

about the red spheres
that bloom inside each
as though brains could flower.
Their insides seem to tremble . . .

Fear . . . that great reminder
that I am, I am still breathing.
Their sclerotic bells and stinging cells
dry out in the insidious sun.

Some jellyfish are the size
of a glass marble, others a fingernail,
smaller even. How they glow
like lost Atlantean coins.

Wherever I look I witness
little endings. Nearly standing
in a husk the size of a dinner plate
I flee the scene through marram grass

and track sticky damp sand
all the way to Buadan's Well
which is said to have healed
those with great sadness.

My neck reaches over
to observe an inviting dark,
some shimmering water
disturbed only by my tears.

Keeper

To my memory, I was always on a Gaelic pitch
in autumn, the trees low and big brown mounds
of leaves. A spectrum of brown thrown in the air
by balls skimming the tops like a scalping razor.

Relegated to the goalposts — those strong legs —
of the better team, I watch, amazed, as they
run, roll and weave as brave as otters, an owl
watching them play. With my end of the pitch

often vacant and shout-less I would busy myself
with the gravel stones beneath me, articulating
them lovingly into stone palaces around the posts.
I wanted to inhabit each one and feel at home.

My father leans on the sideline without a cap,
the autumn chill not so unmanageable yet.
His bald head, like the scored ground under
a wooden swing where wildflowers have a chance.

He begins to yell *Mícheál, Mícheál* and not in
disappointment or embarrassment as I thought
immediately, but to pull me from reverie
as the leather ball whirled towards my cheek.

The rasp in his voice not due to my softness,
I learned years later. No, it was how he lay
witness to a great pain careening towards me
through the cold air, and could not catch it.

Encounter

In Rathmines for a tissue-thin reason —
say helping a friend move boxes —
the clock hand edges toward a given time.

The flower stalls along Grafton Street pour
colour into the brown brick, seasonal tulip tones,
bending sideways from thirst.

What a thrill to know dangerously little,
but how good a buzzcut suits a glass-sharp face.
A tuxedo is only good for the taking off.

Sparkling wine in hand, en route to a grotty
one-bed, he attempts to climb a rakish birch,
leafless. Barely higher than two metres.

I watch silently, deflating as the Prosecco warms.
The tree eventually breaks open under his efforts.
I recall how I once walked away fearlessly.

Keen for A—

after 'Caoineadh Airt Uí Laoghaire' by Eibhlín Dubh Ní Chonaill

Mo chara go daingean tú!
Do thug mo shúil aire duit,
Do thug mo chroí taitneamh duit
Agus d'éalaíos óm charaid leat.
Is domsa nárbh aithreach

> *My hero, my firmest faith,*
> *I recall first taking you in*
> *that cold morning at the mart.*
> *My entire being rose.*
> *I left all I had to follow you.*

Mo ghrá go daingean tú!

My man. My hope.

1 I WAKE TO THE CITY SOUNDING

An evil orange light accompanies 3 a.m. to find me
awake and alone. A— absent, as are those pointed
monochrome dancing shoes. Nothing unusual,
so to speak. A gingham tie hangs from a bedpost;

empty bottles of fragrance; scattered *Will & Grace*
DVDs; a camp gnome; an unblinded window that
remains clear, letting in this frightening night light.
Its clarity is a novelty given how often it fogs

from the combined heat of two men; A— often
in holey boxers and a deep love for unconsciousness.
Faint *wee-woos* of armoured cars and pulses
of some eighteen-year-old's techno soundtrack

my wakening. I can't quite articulate how I know
something terrible is happening. Light crawls
through the door cracks from the filthy bathroom,
bald and uncompromising; entering it would

reveal too much. Sinking as far back as I can
against the headboard, the absolutely clear light
seemingly brightens. The eyes that are mine
close, and resist for a few more hours the thought

don't be dead, don't be dead, don't be dead.

Lá dá bhfaca thú
ag ceann tí an mhargaidh

> *That thirsty morning I witnessed*
> *your entirety in the bustling market.*

2 WE FIRST MEET. THE EVENING IS UNCOMPLICATED

I could barely keep my eyes off you
across the entire stretch of Union Street.
October's sadness had descended,
and the streets lined with ghosts
and slowly rotting pumpkins. You.
The first time I perceived your thighs!
Piano-wire tight and teasingly clothed
in slacks the dainty cream of daisies . . .

Your face flushed beneath the propane heater
or by the prospect of my attention
(wishful thinking), we exchanged words
at the glittery bar counter. Some beer
spilled down your chin, shirt, groin,
and I envied it soaking into your skin.

I knew then that I had discovered the name
of my destination, and would follow you there
along puddled roads and grassy paths
into the meadows in the south of the city,
eventually coming across abandoned Docs,
a pool of clothes, a disturbed surface of water.

Mo ghrá go daingean tú!

My lover, my glowing treasure!

3 KEEN FOR A—

O strong-handed man of mine,

You who could pick me up
with the slightest glance
across the marbled bar,
disco ball glints on pearl buttons,
and lift of your chin, gesturing
to the heavy wood door.
Outside is unsure, various,
so we go without speaking.
Our walk home is punctuated
by you hurling me against doors,
shutters, shaded entryways.
The tang of bergamot lingers
on your collar. Woodsmoke
mixed with cigarettes
strongest in your mouth
which my tongue savoured
and greedily drank.

Mo chara thú go daingean!

My breath.

4 WHAT A— DID

walked by water / spoke kindly to children / never made his intellect a blunt weapon / walked boot soles into notable ruin / spoke to his mother often despite, well . . . / encouraged laughter as a match encourages flame / kept me ticking.

hiked up a mountain / tramped arid fields for an erstwhile kid / had me not too far from there / disappeared into fog / taught me what *aromatics* mean in a frying pan / drove across the city just to be lit momentarily by festive lights / dressed very well indeed.

rested as he needed to / told the young kids throwing eggs to *away and fuck* without getting pelted / had eyes like browning leaves / genuinely laughed at bigots, big belly laughs / just paid me the most extraordinary company.

Mo chara thú go daingean!

My heart.

5 WORD REACHES ME OF A—'S DEATH

Man dear,

The sirens were for you. To think I returned
to sleep while on a patchily-lit street

you bled and your face slowly fell inwards;
my phone begins to light intermittently, then

more regularly, constantly, waking me wide
with the awful absence on your side of the bed.

I knew then. The unused pillow startling
and cold. Chrysanthemums, sequinned thread.

My heart fills and empties in painful pulses
as I take three leaps. One over your side

of the red bed, another to find a loop of keys,
a third falling against my car in 4 a.m. light.

I invent here. In reality I did not bound
to find a first aid kit or a long leather cape,

but I sat still for a very long time on our bed
where last night you lay playing with my hair.

Man dear . . .

do chuid fola leat 'na sraithibh;
is níor fhanas le hí ghlanadh
ach í ól suas lem basaibh.

> *Jesus. You lay in your blood*
> *and I couldn't clean your face.*
> *My hands cup it and I drink red.*

Mo ghrá go daingean tú!

Love. Guiding light.

6 A—'s blood. A—'s clothes

My friend, my sore love,

The policewoman's hands squelch
against the clear plastic baggie
loaded with your clothes,
saturated and drowned in blood.
A cream leather wristwatch.
The gas card with £30 on it.

Later I unzip the damp ruby bag
and eventually empty each item.
Not as damp as I thought, rather
stiff as though they've been starched.
Soft green plaid, your final outfit
stained puce in part, mostly black.

Through retches I lower to them
and smell the frightening copper
decaying the shirt fibres, then
place my lips to where your heart
had protested. Love,
your dried blood marks my mouth.

Mo ghrá go daingean tú!

My one hope.

7 APPEAL FROM BED

Waking early today into blue morning
I happen across a great revelation: denial.
If time, as a book told me, is arrested
then the leaves will never abandon trees,
the milk refuses to curdle, and your face
stays pink and blooming, refutes decay.

Polishing plates, wiping down counters,
even dusting blinds, cutting flowers
for gauche crystal vases you pilfered.
All this in service of your return, whenever
that is, whenever you see fit to find your way.

As this cold evening will now never end
and the morning visitors will never come
I have much empty time to sit silently in,
so I begin to wash clean plates, '70s bowls,

bleach cups more ivory than your skin.
Each scrub another knot in this rope
of my disbelief. I pray every afternoon

that you too are refusing this awful fate.
Otherwise I'll remain alone, and done for.

Is aisling trí néallaibh
do deineadh aréir dom

*You visited me in sleep, friend,
as the witching hour came over.*

8 SKETCH OF A DREAM

A long walk; sharply cold day.
The sky unforgivingly soft-blue.

Dwelling poplars trail over
the flowing surface of river.

A chickpea salad later. Wine.
Album you like. Undressing.

Your seed inside me. Night
outside passing by quietly.

Sleep. Rousing. Turn off alarm.
This glass of water reflects your doze.

Glaofaidh said ar a n-athair

No matter how hard those boys hunt . . .

9 THE CHILDREN FROM NEXT DOOR ARE RINGING THE DOORBELL

Where's A—? they chorus *Where's A—?*
Where's A—? they demand, I think it too

and the chipped wall clock remarks
that I am taking a long time to answer,

hesitating on the last stair. Defiant,
they ring again. What will I tell them, love?

Infamous for your humour, these kids
are in the pursuit of jokes and instead

are greeted by a dark house, curtains
shut. The interior has the quality of dusk

despite the misty but clear morning.
It has been two weeks now. I open the door

to their expectant red faces. *Where's A—?*
Love, those rascals are calling for you.

Won't you come back to appease them?
That evening I stare at the old fairground

mechanical horse you found on eBay
with cheeks that blare red when coins drop in.

40

You found this for them especially.
Each evening you lifted the animatronic

and put it on the front step for those children.
You could make people happy very easily.

Mo chara thú go daingean!

Love of all loves!

10 TENSE

Kneeling onto soft earth, greedy from
the rainfall, I struggle to pinpoint
when the person underfoot evanesced
out of living anecdote and story into that
tense which holds death by the collar.

While the magpies thrust from *here*
to *were here*, and our shoulders
go from dry to burdened, you have been
quietly travelling to the past tense, and
no one noticed, until you had arrived there.

do chuid fola leat 'na sraithibh;
is níor fhanas le hí ghlanadh
ach í ól suas lem basaibh.

> *Love, your blood is the foreground,*
> *seeping into it. Black muck on your face.*
> *I take as much of you into me as I can.*

11 REGARDING A—'S KILLER

1 *Rage*

I imagine the thin-wristed villain
who wrested you out of the world:
faceless, formless; one limb
of a many-armed monster of Provos

or homophobes. All I can picture
is cruelly veined forearms forcing
your soft skin to split and part
again and again. A disembodied grin,

yellowed dog teeth. Barking
Fenian? Faggot? I will light a fire each night
on the Giant's Ring outside the city
and this animal will heed my signal.

On their form I will inflict
every injury, profound and grievous.
Cleave each weasel eye
from the socket, parade their corpse

through the city streets; eat
their cold flesh, revel in their life ending,
and burn and ruin and cut apart
any living thing poisoned by them.

That is my promise.

2 *What comes after (Nothing)*

The house falls dark. The electric has run out, and I'm too ghostly to replenish it. Post mortems mean the funeral is delayed. Word is spreading that I'm not receiving visitors; the cat has slept on your side of the bed since, his head dug between the pillow and the lavender sheet. Some of your hair on the hairbrush I smell sometimes. From bed I watch dust settle on the bunch of roses an old boyfriend brought me. People mean well. The roses — almost block colour red, vivacious as Lego — respire beyond my notice, and the hedge of fir outside the window moves tentatively in an inaudible wind. A—'s killer reclines somewhere, alive and watching the same wind along a different part of its journey, perhaps jostling a tree outside his home. Does he consider me? All this time I have to think.

ná raghadh a chodladh 'na seomra
oíche do thórraimh.

> *not one woman would think*
> *of sleeping while your body is laid out.*

12 THE WAKE. A—'S SISTER SPEAKS

to you in your polished wooden box
as though I am not sitting quietly beside.

Her heart is plainly broken, of course it is;
the surface of her still and impenetrable

like those water-meadows that reproduce sky.
What path have you been led down, brother . . .

No one makes any reference to heaven
as they're not sure you'll make it there.

She mumbles a few more hostile remarks
about the city, the area in which we live,

and the unrighteous. She is seeking relief
in her own way. She side-eyes me.

I stand to my full height. Touch her arm.

Is gránna an choir a chur ar ghaiscíoch
comhra agus caipín

> *A horror to witness you like this,*
> *the coffin, your sunken, bruised face.*

13 THE MORNING OF THE FUNERAL

Love, pet,

The metal wind chimes, three or four tied
to boughs of the apple tree, tinkle away

as do the songbirds accompanying them.
A few shocking bunnies leap in the field.

The morning is yellow. The sky is clear.
How do they act as though all is well?

Mara mbeadh an bholgach
is an bás dorcha
is an fiabhras spotaitheach,
bheadh an marc-shlua borb san

> *Were it not for smallpox,*
> *the sores and lesions,*
> *and the spotted fever*
> *the crowds would have surely come . . .*

14 A—'s funeral. plague times

Hero,

Today I was nearly glad
you didn't have to see
how empty the church was
as you were carried in;
that awful echo that means emptiness
and the slightest sound amplified:
*ahem*s muffled behind elbows
birdsong, accidental tinkles
of the bell that denotes transubstantiation
mumbles of the ancient regulars
rosarying without much heed
paid to your well-shaped coffin.
With my hearing unfocused
they become a medieval chant
half prayer, half chorus
imploring, no, begging Christ
bemoaning this chasm between us, A—.
A nonchalant altar boy
provokes the thurible. It catches

and the incense staggers to the rafters
then the suffocating smell.
I may die right here, I could, I'd do anything.

This pew is unoccupied
save for me (and you
I imagine, just to get through).
Your broad-shouldered family
sits a few rows ahead on the other side
unturned — an ocean between us
but a bit of sea swimming
never bothered you and me.
Bless them, they still think my presence
is a bad influence, or an omen.
The other few attendees —
ten or so in black; weary expressions —
view one another
each hack or unshielded mouth
with brittle suspicion.
Such is sickness
a moral kingdom of its own;
my unrepentant desire
for your face your thighs your forearm
a sickness to some too. Ah well.
Amen, amen, amen
Mother of God. Mother of A—
stands as the priest lumbers in
through the creaking sacristy door.
Her small well-lined face shakes.
There is indeed pain
great pain in the lives
of the unkind too.

The parish priest
a bulky scarecrow of a man

welcomes the few of us gathered
(the whole island would come
if they knew . . .)
he smells like brimstone
before he mentions it.
He raises the book
which he cannot venerate
with the traditional kiss
given the plague outside.
He opens the book
and puffs his chest, blessing
the words, blessing us
but certainly not *us*, A—.
How inadequate are these prayers
uttered in squalid caves
millennia ago
attempting to articulate a grief
a desire a life
they had no comprehension of.
I am writing this phantasm
as their mumbles and respectable wishes
do not encapsulate us. Forgive me
love, this is hard.
He begins to read from the book.

That voice fills the cavern
like water filling a barrel
I'm being drowned in.
The dust flints in sunlight
above his head, halo-ish
the cobwebs catch gold.
The thick pillar candles
recall you, flickering
long, melting under heat
soon extinguished.

He reads Leviticus first.
If a man lies with a man
as he does a woman
he discovers anal orgasm
you used to say.
When people like us
are sentenced to death
the priestly prophet exclaims
our blood is upon us.
I think of your blood
and how it warmed my lips
vibrant and already cold.
Your blood is within me
and I keep it safe.
If that love is abomination
I'm comforted by the thought
I'll join you soon enough.
Hero, I need saving
from this from your silent family
from this faux-wise cleric
from your absence.

He reads from Revelations next.
The cowardly akin to murderers,
the faithless, the sexually immoral, the sorcerers,
this is our inheritance.
A— bathes in this lake of fire.
This is *the second death*
the priest concludes
closing over the book.
Momentary hope!
Were it that this oak-box affair
was your first
a lucky escape.
Were this the case

I'd knowingly follow
an empty coffin
down the nave of the church
then the stone vestibule
anticipating you outside
relishing the morning
your second chance
where you will throw off disguise
grab my person
close the books we spent our days in
and run into the adjoining fields
never ever stopping going.

do chuid fola leat 'na sraithibh;
is níor fhanas le hí ghlanadh
ach í ól suas lem basaibh.

> *Blood puddle. Clouds of blood.*
> *I wake sometimes with the taste.*
> *Your blood is all I have left.*

15 WHAT I HEAR FROM A—'S FAMILY IN THE WEEKS AFTER

Mo ghrá go daingean tú!

My love! My affectionate calf!

16 CALF BY A—'S GRAVE. SIX MONTHS AFTER

Love,

The evening bristles with a fine mizzle
as I come to visit you. Still no grass
over your head, but this bare bald mound
drinks as much rain as it can bear.

Bunches of heal-alls skirt your perimeter.
I consider shovelling them all into my mouth.
Later a webpage outlines that these purple
wildflowers are also called heart-of-the-earth.

A troupe of brown and fair cows munch
grass (and healing herbs!) in the adjacent field,
and a calf — with a semi-circle of fair hair
that suggests a glamorous full fringe —

pauses from its evening constitutional
around the limits of its hilly patch to watch
me watch you. Some leaves and stems fall
from its ajar mouth. Like a bolt it bolts

half a field away, as though what it saw
or what I was seeing were unbearable.

stoca chúig dhual duit,
buatais go glúin ort

those cambric tights,
those thigh-high boots of yours . . .

17 WARDROBE THRESHOLD. A—'S SMELL

Denim jackets, jeans, a short-sleeved denim shirt you wore that first afternoon. An odorous check shirt you stuffed in the back rather than wash, soft brushed cotton. Even your reek is favourable to anything else. Tank tops, more than I can count. A fringe jacket. Some hats fall off the hook nailed to the internal side of the sliding door. The cowboy hat you wore one Hallowe'en. A bent grey sword from that same October. A favourite yellow beanie. Some hair. I place each piece of clothing in my hands like the Eucharist and thank God for these visitations.

fola

*Blood. Bloodshed. Bloody sweat.
Blood was stirred. Streaming
blood. Blue blood. Blood vomit.
Blood drained from his cheeks.
Dripping blood. Hot blooded.
Blood feud. Blood boiling.
Giving blood to the soil.
Baptism by blood.
Spirit of blood. Bloodberry.
Eruption of blood. Bloodless.
Bloodthirst.*

18 FORENSIC REPORT

1 *Ten months after the death*

Findings remain
inconclusive; who
is to say *why*.
But *how?* That
it may suggest:

his aorta
was transected —
a vessel
that accompanied A—
through years —
and he was found

by a nurse
on her way to the night shift.
Saw the puddle growing . . .
He was breathing
very laboriously,
despite being gone.

It is not unusual
for respiration to persist
minutes after
the heart has ceased.
Take another breath,
one more, just one more —

2 *Photos of the incident are offered to me*

In a warehouse
somewhere in the region
exists a database
in a filing cabinet

with photos of people
and their last moments
crystallized, like a raindrop
in a shutter snap.

Actually torn asunder;
bullets parting them;
fused with car dashboards,
almost at peace.

Your portraits rest
in a manila envelope
I misplace on purpose.
Unopenable. Your face . . .

May this warehouse
be razed to the ground,
and all of this
awful grief with it.

Mo ghrá go daingean tú!

My surest footing.

19 A—'s friends gather in the traditional way

A warm day indeed, the sky lit dying orange
by a somewhat eclipsed sun, and on this day

we choose to meet in the coffee shop
my surest footing often walked himself to.

What a curiosity! The grey business suits thought,
all these men in a circle in different coloured clothes

*chewing over a memory, then lowering their heads
onto the wooden table to sob and sob and sob.*

Mo ghrá go daingean tú!

Partner.

20 A YEAR PASSES. BLACKBERRY SEASON

The brambles scratch my legs, encroaching
onto the pavement, burdened with berries
that bob purple-black the size of bird hearts.
Certain drupelets are ruptured by, I presume,

insects that subsequently enjoyed a bloodbath.
The first loosens between these two fingers
and stains awfully. A sweet kiss, I think,
and go to pick another when a louse falls

from the rafters of the bramble, tumbling
away into the green-brown bank of the river.
I remove this louse's half-chewed berry bed
from my mouth, and begin to jog home.

I spit a shockingly red juice into the overgrowth
as if I've been socked, bleeding internally.
A passerby might think me fleeing harm,
bent over and panting with a purple-black mouth.

I learned this year that *púca*s piss on berries
on Michaelmas, naturally dodgy to eat after,
and, on finding this funny, I think to tell you,
realize, try to remember your laugh.

Is éirigh suas id' sheasamh

Get up. Shake off this coldness.

21 INVOCATION

Oh my bright-eyed friend, man dear,

A—, my memory of you
refuses to fade, even cluttered
as I am with receipts, pens,
newly acquired phone numbers.

This remembering
sustains me (my hope
for your grand return); return
from this vanishing act.

Yes . . . not dead but *vanished*,
from which I can hear footsteps,
proof of ongoingness, even
if it is far, far from me.

If you will not return
to these fields that spew
flowers for us: be well,
drink cold water, remember

the life we fashioned
against extraordinary odds;
how we thought the church bell
soundtrack to our walks.

And with all this said, all of it,
I cannot abandon the sense

that you will beat me home,
feet up, sun lightening your eyes.

Sheep Chorus, Lisheegan

Even toward midnight the surrounding fields bleat discord.
I sit against the stippled wall by the opaque square window.

A gargoylesque moth, peppered but mostly white across the thorax,
hovers around an outside light, a votive, humming something.

The sheep chorus quietens as though also fascinated
by this white corpse of a vibrating moth. Yes, a white corpse . . .

or a husk of a body entirely drained of blood, yes . . . better . . .
Somewhere out there a small stream cuts through the field

like an assassin with good intentions . . . And perhaps the sheep,
Cladoirs, Galways and Cheviots, roar some lost language . . .

A sudden girl with rings of golden hair sits beside me.
I feel newly self-conscious, *what to liken things to* . . .

but she pauses sagely and looks out the dark window.
Baaaaa, she says. *They go baaaaa*. I had forgotten.

She is five, and still free from words meaning anything
beyond now. One more time . . . A sheep with one cyan mark lingers

by the well-hammered fence. The barbed-wire loops
look dangerous. Muck darkens its white underside.

It stands a little apart from its flock — friends? siblings?
How have we been hurt that this must mean something else.

Were it that words were sufficient. Were it that they
could save us, and were no momentary crossing to safety.

Swimming Off Snave Pier

And the length of a stolen week
against my better judgement
I step from the disguise of clothes
to be dressed round by a cold wind,

then move snail-slow into that
unbelievably open green sea
the childish colour of money.
The chill so awful my stomach

distends like a big beach stone,
then less awful, then actually fine.
Oh a blessing to be out of my depth,
the awful weight not gone but changed.

Whiddy Island bobs in and out of sight.
A big umbrella of a jellyfish beside me.
For a minute or two I focus entirely
on keeping afloat, free from metaphor.

Offshore Wind Farm

A particularly still day to be taken
through the sky at an aeroplane's pace

when I notice thousands of feet underneath
how they rise from the North Sea, archipelago

of monuments that, on this particularly still
morning, provide a perch for tired seabirds

to dry off and catch their breath. The still
windmills: a drowned gravesite, an inscription

we tried to fix things while we could. From here
they seem close together but so much separates them . . .

I am happy lately, and think of these instruments
of harnessing — soaked to the skin, lonely —

from a point so high above the cloud bank.
They have halted turning and are taking stock.

The one furthest out into the sea, dislocated
from its colleagues and in the deepest water,

desires warmth and a knowing look. That's all.
These windmills have little trouble stilling

on this particularly clear day where the offing
is a starling egg. When you and I are alone,

as the night gets on with itself,
as the angry Labrador defends its perimeter,

we sit together quietly by one lamplight
watching the leaves drift, half-hear the radio . . .

Plane smashes into the scarified concrete
and, as my belt clasp opens, I forget their lesson

and, on barrelling past the luggage carousel,
busy, busy, busy, my happiness remains in the air.

In a Lover's Family's Company

My forehead warms against
the shield of your shoulder
in a noisy people-carrier
while I hunt for
a reluctant belt buckle.

For just a moment I linger
slightly irritated
by scratchy wool,
feeling your pulse throb
through your bicep.

It comforted me,
this amateur embrace.
You caught my eye briefly,
then turned to your nephew,
the atmosphere untroubled.

Seemingly cursory,
certainly to your family,
maybe even to you.
A thieved intimacy,
a night in a balmy harbour.

Here is our inheritance:
the sound of rushing water
for those without ears to hear
all the tiny water creatures
below, quartz in our gills.

Late Blight

The field had spent years drinking
rain and pills, received infusions, dialysis,
pesticide repair. Now Creeslough breathes again.
Its scarred mouth opened, sleep furry.
The field is threaded through for the new
harvest, overwintered. The lambs,
heartily wooled, bounce over orange soil
to find a newer water, frost-hardy.
Some were quick-footed. Some came back later,
others love this image: their children alive;
young ones loving cappuccinos. The field
understood, knew they had to flock elsewhere,
busy re-stitching its rooty intestine networks.

Years later the field, mid-Rosary, was visited.
Two boys in soil-brown dungarees, one leading
the other by the hand. Not disturbing
the braided potato ridges they skirted the edges
and disappeared into a thin wood. *Fuck
my mouth* hears the field, and in response
hopes they'll stay. It has pierced its ears
with helleborine and blue-eyed grass.
The boys come out from the trees
eventually, holding their cans like prayer beads.
Come back home, says the field.
Some beer is spilled generously for the field.
I'm awake! it says, reeling.

Devotion

I ROMANCE OPTION

for Eva Griffin

I direct my avatar in circles and rings
around the desires of a bohemian mage who
addresses me handsomely and hotly as 'thou'
or 'I blush as a stream bleeds red at sunset
seeing your figure appearing in my chambers'.
I hope to impress and make myself necessary,
and just for now I am the only one who knows
that I am pursuing a lithe man, that a world

trembles — uniquely mine — sealed by incantations
and decisions that will be remembered later.
The evening birds peep blearily in the loud hedge
of forest flame, and that I play at myself in secret
is no concern to them, and I return to enchanting.
Praise these vessels, rafts to a peopled island.

2 WHY THE CAT MEANS WHAT IT DOES

for Martina Evans

Because he is the one thing I don't have to justify myself to.

Because he wets his paws to clean his forehead with such care
    I am reminded of the pleasures of duty.

Because he shows kindness to me and is shrewd with strangers.

Because the evening I drove to get him off the Shankill the night
    was black and unforgiving, and he rose from a puddle
    of his siblings to grant me an audience.

Because electing to love something you don't have to means
    something.

Because I refuse to bend to the Christian neighbour's conception
    of a meaningful life. Because he hissed at her.

Because another neighbour assumed we were brothers who
    shared a cat.

Because people think he is just a cat, and neglect to consider how
    a gold band is anything but a symbol, and are wrong.

Because when the front door opens he peels his paw in the jamb
    to pry the door open quicker as though he were a monk
    in pursuit of a long-awaited word that made him think
    ah, how good to find a new word for love.

Because the room was full of music only I liked, and he
    brushed his cheeks on the legs of my chair and sat with
    me a while.

Because he lies beside me and guides my eyes to the window.

Because if it is well with his soul it should be with mine.

Because around eleven every morning when I am drowsy and unhappy he meows quietly and lies on the floral bedspread.

Because I so rarely hear, *I need you. I need you.*

3 ENVOI

These empty and agonized nights
you retire early; I sit up for matins.
Outside the premature daffodils bow
their papery, trembling shoulders.

Instead night and I have hooked up,
bosom-buddies, collegial hecklers,
but most often we listen. A small-
sounding dog bark. Coming wind.

If I pretend, I can hear the calm tide
of your breath a few rooms over
as reassuring as a remarkable clock
when I really hear a colossal quiet.

I spend the rest of tonight's lateness
wishing I were brave enough to pull you
back into life, encourage us outside
where the soft mizzle, where the moon . . .

4 IMPROMPTU EVENING

Shed these bedclothes! Pull apart
the dirty cream curtains! We spill
out beneath a bald, dimming sky
in search of an affordable meal.
We talk on the embankment walk.
The year has been unforgiving.
The songbirds have not yet
returned to the hedge outside.

I spread a red pepper tapenade
over the tiger bread, masticating
like a tiger. Some napa slaw lipsticks
your mouth. I motion, you wipe.
You daub some herb oil on bread,
eat, your eyes widen, then wrinkle.
Were I to die before morning
this would have been enough.

5 LOVE POEM

for Andrew Cunning

The only person with a grasp of my language,
who from one look can divine I'm saying *Raid
the cupboards for all the tramadol you can find.*

You of lithe frame and libraried mind, whose company —
even in silence or sleep — brings such clarity,
whose cheeks split in laughter are a great thing.

A life is spent encountering bin lid after bin lid
engorged on their book learning and *'achievements'*.
The cat preens himself of an evening, unbothered.

I will happily count my life in the story of each day
I tell you every evening, our faces close
and the outside leering in the square window.

Love and death are our inexhaustible topics.
The poets are unanimous. I pity them, though, never
knowing how your cheeks shine when you really laugh.

20s

A grandmother bends
over a leather apothecary satchel
occupied by the queue of remedies
required by the townsfolk,
yet her daughter's child
desires a bedtime analogy.
She drops sorrel and bog rosemary
into the mortar, then turns kindly
to the young girl peering
through a curtain of dark hair.

*There was a great flood long ago
which shocked the townspeople.
The doctor and headsman and sage watched in silence.
Buildings lifted from their foundations
and drifted themselves down the thoroughfare —
blue-green water — out of sight
like the cocksure ones who follow the sun.
Lucky those who were gathering strawberries
on the valley sides. The ephemera of the town
bobbed like a train along the newly formed river.*

The astronomer's ephemeris, a child's toy woven from straw . . .
Granddaughter lay disturbed in her bed,
newly alert to the assassin water, convinced
she would wake into a new blue world.
I'm frightened for what's to come.
The grandmother rubs her feet.
*Some survived. My own grandmother
was one. She looked around at those few
still there, shivering and close by, and thought
it could be worse.*

How We Got Here, Where We're Going

for Mary Montague

In the dimly lit undergrowth
of a Central American rainforest
jewel-like
male hummingbirds

flit through the vegetation,
pausing briefly to mate
now with a male,
now with a female.

Drifting off to sleep,
two male monkeys
lie gently
in each other's arms.

In a protected New Zealand inlet
a pair of female gulls —
mated for life —
tend their chicks together.

Circling and prancing
around her partner
a female antelope courts
another female

in an ageless,
elegant
ritual staged
on the African savannah.

On every continent
animals of the same sex

seek each other out,
doing so for millions of years.

They court each other,
using intricate and beautiful
mating dances —
result of eons of evolution.

Being Naked with Strangers

The shower at home has been shorn from the wall
for weeks at this point, so stripping off in company
has become second nature. I make imaginary pals
with the GAA lads and finance guy who talk seriously

about kilograms and artificial protein, seemingly
oblivious to my placid undressing beside them.
The changing room smells inoffensive at this early
hour, and they discuss the day, politics, STEM

not needing women, and I silently undress
and unroll like a busted mattress, clothes puddling.
LED lights leave no bulge unattended to, stress
each groaning waistband or muscle rivulet convulsing.

Alongside these men I have no place beside
I take my place in the line for the uncurtained shower —
— why is *this* a fantasy? — feeling strangely astride
these moustached men, easily nude, who tower

over me like a building. Under hot water I wonder
if wisdom is knowing skin is nothing to be afraid of.
Maybe I will someday want to be alive, stunned,
as this West Belfast man desires to 'grow' himself.

No towel-snapping or adolescent flashbacks
beneath this nacreous morning. Just four of us moving
beyond the night before. One touches my back
and asks for shampoo. He smiles. I am shaking.

Travelling Poem

Planes the size of friends leave the city
in swathes, what feels daily these days.
My mother and I drink coffee wincing
as each colourful flight roars overhead.
The black coffee is bitter. Goodbye . . .

A shame, Mammy says, all they'll miss,
gesturing to the delicate white blooms
of a tree hanging lithely over a blue car,
or perhaps she means this place,
the fire and words and people between

the thin flowers and this stone balcony.
She is wise in this regard, having shredded
papers and ambition to play a violin
all across a life. The radio's frequency
favours the music of elsewhere.

The best part of a decade has been given
to my roots sinking into this damp soil
in knowledge that difficulty remains difficult
by a poolside or a municipal park.
Arrival is just a feeling

that comes in those broad seconds
in an unfamiliar place where clarity
meets strangeness, like that morning
on Baggot Street where the canal stilled
and Charlotte linked my arm

where the sky cleared grey into blue
and Kavanagh sat observing the rushes.
Arrival is attention, and each morning
I arrive to my mother thinking of me.
I drive to see her. Life is fragrant.

To an Imagined Child

Friends of certain militant dispositions would have kittens
    hearing me address you like this.

To have a child, they say, is a heterosexual fallacy!
    There's enough tragedy

on this drowning world without a replica of me
    making matters worse. And yet

book-learning crumbles in the face of a child's toy,
    a small pink hairbrush.

I dream of you to the soft cluck of knitting needles.
    You would know me

always in the same coat, waiting outside the school
    well before I had to.

Maybe some part of us is meant to be weighed down,
    I might say to my friends.

A diving line is often deployed in murky caves so a diver
    can ascend to gentle water.

Child, I would stand still with this line around my trunk
    in the shallow water

of our lives, so that you can tug twice for *I'm okay,*
    I'm okay, Daddy,

go well into your own life and stand among flowers
    you cannot grow

and smile knowing that wherever I go you follow
    as a prayer follows hope.

Walking Through Empty Houses

Receiving the customary
chill passing Paisley's church —
a theological spank
on the bottom —

we are soon greeted
as two brothers
by the gilet-wound
estate agent.

He struggles to turn
his BMW
cobalt and sleek
in the tiny cul-de-sac.

A writer, is it?
BMW asks if you are proud
and I wonder does he
refer to *our* mother.

Somewhere in Ballysillan
seems promising.
Then three articles unspool
of Catholic families

'prevented' from moving in.
'Not too West, not too East.'
For the first time
I wish my namesake away.

Packs of miserable people,
a kettle of vultures awaiting
Susie the estate agent
to disembark her Micra.

Poor Susie, friendly
but without *enough*
hunks of meat
for all the jet-black jackals

with our red eyes ...
She unlocks the bright
pink door — perfect for
poofs, I say; you frown —

and desperate people
abandon small cars
and umbrellas.
We speak quietly

as we step through
a small terraced house
as though on consecrated ground
where we don't belong.

Having endured the last
what's for you
well-wish, I go catatonic
in Buoy Park.

Simple are my requests.
To cook eggs well
on a stove I inherit
while looking out to a yard

painted mint green —
pebbles in terracotta pots
from which nasturtiums erupt
and crawl the walls.

To lie in bed and watch
a stippled ceiling.
Sounds of kids tumbling up
and down the stairs next door

rather than paramilitaries
kicking the other men
out of the house next door.
For the lock to be strong,

the windows to be open,
a front door to be painted
a lively colour,
to be undisturbed

with my cat
on a cheap upright.
For those squares of sun
on the rug to be mine.

Unaccompanied Walk

Abandoning shade only
for the cool of 10 p.m.,
the light dimming with the heat.
Trees, dirt paths, wildflowers

loosen into silhouette.
Maybe monks struggled
to abandon their copybooks
and open their doors too.

Cow parsley and ox-eye
daisies object into my path
alongside the quiet river.
Blessèdly alone.

Pipistrelles are so numerous
or else one particularly enjoys my company.
My eyes flit upwards
half-glimpsing them twist and barrel.

It is as though
they walk with me, share
a common need to look
on water going, going.

It is buttercup season
which reminds me it is no longer
magnolia season. The pink
petals of the one I love

part of the lawn's language now —
I sat under them
and was happy. I will again.
I gather flowers and walk home.

Acknowledgements and Notes

Acknowledgements are due to the editors of the following publications where some of these poems, or versions of them, were published first: *Cyphers, Fourteen Publishing, The Manchester Review, Poetry Ireland Review* and *Skein Press*. I was fortunate to spend a period of time with Leontia Flynn and owe her an enormous debt, as I do to Peter Fallon for his careful attention to this book. I am grateful to those who have spent time with these poems before they became this book, and for their time and insight: Andrew Cunning, Sonya Gildea, Charles Lang, Bebe Ashley, Ellen Orchard, Eva Griffin, William Keohane and Charlotte Buckley.

- *page* 13 This poem renders the Biblical scene where Mary Magdalene encounters Christ's tomb empty, and mistakes the resurrected Christ for a gardener. It echoes a line from 'The Boy' by Marie Howe.
- *page* 15 This is a translation from the Irish of the anonymous c. 9th-century poem 'Pangur Bán', most likely attributed to an Irish monk on or near Reichenau Island, Germany. The original Irish for this poem, as well as 'Líadan Attests Her Love', comes from *Early Irish Lyrics* (ed. Gerard Murphy, Clarendon Press, 1956).
- *page* 22 On 9 May 1997 Darren Bradshaw, a gay RUC policeman, was killed by an INLA gunman in Belfast's then only gay bar, The Parliament.
- *page* 24 This poem adapts its first line from a poem in W H Auden's *Look, Stranger!* (Faber and Faber, 1936); the title acknowledges how Auden, by obliquely referring to his male love object as 'you', somehow evaded homophobic scrutiny.
- *page* 30 A re-telling of *Caoineadh Airt Uí Laoghaire* by Eibhlín Dubh Ní Chonaill. The Irish fragments have been reproduced from Pádraig Feirtéar's transcription, found in University College Dublin's Special Collections. I am indebted to Angela Bourke for her scholarship and to Vona Groarke for her razor-sharp thinking around this poem and for her support.

page 78 A found poem from Bruce Bagemihl's *Biological Exuberance: Animal Homosexuality and Natural Diversity* (St. Martin's Press, 1999), and the poem itself is indebted to Mary Montague's expertise and friendship.

page 87 This poem is for Evelyn Wilson and in the fond memory of spending time around that blue hydrangea bush that isn't there anymore.